30-MINUTE MEALS

Contents

Welcome!

Not only am I a dedicated and enthusiastic cook, but I love nothing more than encouraging those who think they are domestically challenged to pick up a pan and a spoon and get stirring. It doesn't take much to grasp the basics and from there, anything is possible. Hiding behind the mantra 'I can't cook' only brings fear into the kitchen, but it is these mistakes that will ultimately make you a better, more confident and knowledgeable cook. All it takes is some good recipes and plenty of enthusiasm and kitchen domination will surely follow. Luckily, all Good Housekeeping cookery books are filled with tempting recipes with clear methods and realistic photography – we are taking the chance out of cooking as our recipes are guaranteed to work.

If you have ever tried turning the page of a cookery book with dirty hands, while also balancing a steaming pan and a sticky spoon, then you will love the flip-chart design of this book. The simple fact that the recipes stand upright makes for an easier cooking experience – say goodbye to hovering over recipes while trying to stop the spoon dripping on to the pages.

This Good Housekeeping Flip It! book collection is filled with meticulously triple-tested recipes that have been developed and put through their paces in our dedicated test kitchens. We hope you enjoy the recipes and that they inspire you to give them a try – you know that they'll work after all!

Meike.

Cookery Editor
Good Housekeeping

Classic Omelette

Serves 1
Preparation Time
5 minutes
Cooking Time
5 minutes

Per Serving
449 calories
40g fat
(of which 19g saturates)
1g carbohydrate
1g salt

Vegetarian

2–3 medium eggs
1 tbsp milk or water
25g (1oz) unsalted butter
salt and ground black pepper
sliced or grilled tomatoes and
freshly chopped flat-leafed
parsley to serve

1 Whisk the eggs in a bowl, just enough to break them down – over-beating spoils the texture of the omelette. Season with salt and pepper, and add the milk or water.

2 Heat the butter in an 18cm (7in) omelette pan or non-stick frying pan until it is foaming, but not brown. Add the eggs and stir gently with a fork or wooden spatula, drawing the mixture from the sides to the centre as it sets and letting the liquid egg in the centre run to the sides. When set, stop stirring and cook for 30 seconds or until the omelette is golden brown underneath and still creamy on top: don't overcook. If you are making a filled omelette, add the filling at this point.

3 Tilt the pan away from you slightly and use a palette knife to fold over one-third of the omelette to the centre, then fold over the opposite third. Slide the omelette out on to a warmed plate, letting it flip over so that the folded sides are underneath. Serve immediately, with tomatoes sprinkled with parsley.

Roasted Vegetable Tartlets

Makes 6
Preparation Time
15 minutes
Cooking Time
about 7 minutes

Per Tartlet
356 calories
24g fat
(of which 1g saturates)
30g carbohydrate
1.1g salt

Vegetarian

375g pack ready-rolled puff pastry, thawed
if frozen
plain flour to dust
1 medium egg, beaten
2 tbsp coarse sea salt
300g (11oz) vegetable antipasti in olive oil
olive oil, if needed
2 tbsp balsamic vinegar
190g tub red pepper hummus
50g (2oz) wild rocket
salt and ground black pepper

1. Preheat the oven to 220°C (200°C fan oven) mark 7. Unroll the puff pastry on a lightly floured surface and cut it into six squares. Put the pastry squares on a large baking sheet and prick each one all over with a fork. Brush the surface with beaten egg and sprinkle the edges with sea salt. Bake for 5–7 minutes until the pastry is golden brown and cooked through. Press down the centre of each tartlet slightly with the back of a fish slice.

2. Make the dressing. Pour 4 tbsp oil from the jar of antipasti into a bowl (top it up with a little more olive oil if there's not enough in the antipasti jar). Add the vinegar, season with salt and pepper and mix well, then put to one side.

3. To serve, spread some hummus over the central part of each tartlet. Put the tartlets on individual plates and spoon on the antipasti – there's no need to be neat. Whisk the balsamic vinegar dressing. Add the rocket leaves and toss to coat, then pile a small handful of leaves on top of each tartlet. Serve immediately.

Get Ahead
To prepare ahead Complete the recipe to the end of step 1. Leave the tartlets to cool on a wire rack, then store in an airtight container. It will keep for up to two days.
To use Complete the recipe.

Broccoli & Goat's Cheese Soup

Serves 6
Preparation Time
10 minutes
Cooking Time
20 minutes

Per Serving
220 calories
16g fat
(of which 10g saturates)
8g carbohydrate
0.5g salt

Vegetarian

50g (2oz) butter
2 medium onions, chopped
1 litre (1¾ pints) vegetable, chicken or turkey stock
700g (1½lb) broccoli, broken into florets, stout stalks peeled and chopped
1 head of garlic, separated into cloves, unpeeled
1 tbsp olive oil
150g (5oz) goat's cheese
salt and ground black pepper

1 Preheat the oven to 200°C (180°C fan oven) mark 6. Melt the butter in a pan over a gentle heat. Add the onions, then cover the pan and cook for 4–5 minutes until translucent. Add half the stock and bring to the boil. Add the broccoli and bring back to the boil, then cover the pan, reduce the heat and simmer for 15–20 minutes until the broccoli is tender.

2 Meanwhile, toss the cloves of garlic in the oil and tip into a roasting tin. Roast in the oven for 15 minutes or until soft when squeezed.

3 Leave the soup to cool a little, then add the goat's cheese and whiz in batches in a blender or food processor until smooth. Return the soup to the pan and add the remaining stock. Reheat gently on the hob and season to taste with salt and pepper.

4 Ladle the soup into warmed bowls, squeeze the garlic out of their skins and scatter over the soup, add a sprinkling of black pepper and serve.

Try Something Different
Double the quantity of goat's cheese, if you prefer a stronger taste.
Instead of goat's cheese, substitute a soft garlic cheese for a really garlicky flavour.

Italian-style Steak Salad

Serves 4
Preparation Time
15 minutes
Cooking Time
5 minutes,
plus resting

Per Serving
378 calories
25g fat
(of which 6g saturates)
3g carbohydrate
1.1g salt

Gluten Free

2 × 250g (9oz) rump steaks, fat trimmed
salt and ground black pepper
1 tbsp extra virgin olive oil, plus extra to drizzle
(optional)
2–3 tbsp fresh pesto, to taste
110g bag salad leaves
250g (9oz) cherry tomatoes
100g (3½oz) marinated artichoke pieces from
a jar, drained
50g (2oz) toasted pinenuts
25g (1oz) Parmesan cheese shavings
crusty bread to serve

1 Pat the steaks dry with kitchen paper, then season well on both sides. Heat the oil in a large frying pan over a high heat and fry the steaks for 5 minutes, turning once, for medium rare (cook for longer or shorter depending on your preference).

2 Meanwhile, in a small bowl, stir together the pesto, some black pepper and enough water to make a loose dressing. Put the salad leaves, tomatoes and artichoke pieces into a large serving bowl, then pour over most of the pesto dressing and toss to combine.

3 When the steaks are cooked, transfer to a board and leave to rest for 5 minutes before slicing into strips. Add the steak strips to the salad, then drizzle over the remaining pesto dressing and some extra oil, if you like. Sprinkle the pinenuts and Parmesan shavings over the top and serve immediately with crusty bread.

Goat's Cheese & Walnut Salad

Serves 6
Preparation Time
10 minutes

Per Serving
428 calories
41g fat
(of which 10g saturates)
3g carbohydrate
0.5g salt

Vegetarian
Gluten Free

1 large radicchio, shredded
2 bunches of prepared watercress,
about 125g (4oz) total weight
1 red onion, finely sliced
150g (5oz) walnut pieces
200g (7oz) goat's cheese, crumbled

For the dressing
2 tbsp red wine vinegar
8 tbsp olive oil
a large pinch of caster sugar
salt and ground black pepper

1 Whisk all the ingredients for the dressing in a small bowl and put to one side.

2 Put the radicchio, watercress and onion into a large bowl. Pour the dressing over the salad and toss well.

3 To serve, divide the salad among six plates and sprinkle the walnuts and goat's cheese on top.

Sprouted Bean & Mango Salad

Serves 6

Preparation Time
15 minutes

Per Serving
103 calories
4g fat
(of which 1g saturates)
15g carbohydrate
0.1g salt

Vegetarian
Gluten Free
Dairy Free

3 tbsp mango chutney
grated zest and juice of 1 lime
2 tbsp olive oil
4 plum tomatoes
1 small red onion, finely chopped
1 red pepper, seeded and finely diced
1 yellow pepper, seeded and finely diced
1 mango, finely diced
4 tbsp freshly chopped coriander
150g (5oz) sprouted beans (see Cook's Tip)
salt and ground black pepper

1 To make the dressing, place the mango chutney in a small bowl and add the lime zest and juice. Whisk in the oil and season.

2 Quarter the tomatoes, discard the seeds and then dice. Put into a large bowl with the onion, peppers, mango, coriander and sprouted beans. Pour the dressing over and mix well. Serve the salad immediately.

Try Something Different
Use papaya instead of mango.
Ginger and chilli dressing Mix together 2 tsp grated fresh root ginger, 1 tbsp sweet chilli sauce, 2 tsp white wine vinegar and 2 tbsp walnut oil. Season with salt.
Peanut dressing Mix together 1 tbsp peanut butter, ¼ crushed dried chilli, 4 tsp white wine vinegar, 3 tbsp walnut oil, 1 tsp sesame oil and a dash of soy sauce.

Cook's Tip
Sprouted beans and seeds are rich in nutrients and lend a nutty taste and crunchy texture to salads and stir-fries. Fresh bean sprouts are available from most supermarkets. Many beans and seeds can be sprouted at home, though it is important to buy ones which are specifically produced for sprouting – from a healthfood shop or other reliable source. Mung beans, aduki beans, alfalfa seeds and fenugreek are all suitable.
Mung beans take five to six days to sprout. Allow 125g (4oz) bean sprouts per person. Rinse bean sprouts well in cold water, then drain. Cook in boiling salted water or steam for 30 seconds, or stir-fry for 1–2 minutes.

Spinach & Goat's Cheese Frittata

Serves 4
Preparation Time
10 minutes
Cooking Time
12 minutes

Per Serving
281 calories
21g fat
(of which 9g saturates)
3g carbohydrate
0.9g salt

Gluten Free

200g (7oz) baby leeks, trimmed and chopped
4 spring onions, chopped
125g (4oz) baby leaf spinach
6 large eggs
4 tbsp milk
freshly grated nutmeg
125g (4oz) soft goat's cheese, chopped
1 tbsp olive oil
salt and ground black pepper
mixed salad leaves to serve

1 Preheat the grill to high. Blanch the leeks in a pan of lightly salted boiling water for 2 minutes. Add the spring onions and spinach just before the end of the cooking time. Drain, rinse in cold water and dry on kitchen paper.

2 Whisk together the eggs, milk and nutmeg. Season with salt and pepper. Stir the goat's cheese into the egg mixture with the leeks, spinach and spring onions.

3 Heat the oil in a non-stick frying pan. Pour in the frittata mixture and fry gently for 4–5 minutes, then finish under the hot grill for 4–5 minutes until the top is golden and just firm. Serve with mixed salad.

Try Something Different
Use a different cheese, such as Stilton.

Mozzarella, Parma Ham & Rocket Pizza

Serves 4
Preparation Time
10 minutes
Cooking Time
15–18 minutes

Per Serving
508 calories
19.1g fat
(of which 10.5g saturates)
64.2g carbohydrate
1.9g salt

a little plain flour to dust
290g pack pizza base mix
350g (12oz) fresh tomato and chilli pasta sauce
250g (9oz) buffalo mozzarella cheese, drained and roughly chopped
6 slices Parma ham, torn into strips
50g (2oz) rocket
a little extra virgin olive oil to drizzle
salt and ground black pepper

1 Preheat the oven to 200°C (180°C fan oven) mark 6 and lightly flour two large baking sheets. Mix up the pizza base according to the pack instructions. Divide the dough into two and knead each ball on a lightly floured surface for about 5 minutes, then roll them out to make two 23cm (9in) rounds. Put each on to the prepared baking sheet.

2 Divide the tomato sauce between the pizza bases and spread it over, leaving a small border around each edge. Scatter over the mozzarella pieces, then scatter with ham. Season well with salt and pepper.

3 Cook the pizzas for 15–18 minutes until golden. Slide on to a wooden board, top with rocket leaves and drizzle with olive oil. Cut in half to serve.

Cook's Tip
If you're short of time, buy two ready-made pizza bases.

Very Easy Four-cheese Gnocchi

Serves 2

Preparation Time
3 minutes

Cooking Time
10 minutes

Per Serving
630 calories
28g fat
(of which 15g saturates)
77g carbohydrate
5.7g salt

Vegetarian
Gluten Free

350g pack fresh gnocchi
300g tub fresh four-cheese sauce
240g pack sunblush tomatoes
2 tbsp freshly torn basil leaves,
plus basil sprigs to garnish
1 tbsp freshly grated Parmesan
(see Cook's Tip)
15g (½oz) butter, chopped
salt and ground black pepper
salad to serve

1 Cook the gnocchi in a large pan of lightly salted boiling water according to the pack instructions, or until all the gnocchi have floated to the surface. Drain well and put the gnocchi back into the pan.

2 Preheat the grill. Add the four-cheese sauce and tomatoes to the gnocchi and heat gently, stirring, for 2 minutes.

3 Season with salt and pepper, then add the basil and stir again. Spoon into individual heatproof bowls, sprinkle a little Parmesan over each one and dot with the butter.

4 Cook under the hot grill for 3–5 minutes until golden and bubbling. Garnish with basil sprigs and serve with salad.

Cook's Tip
Traditional Parmesan cheese contains animal rennet, but you can now buy vegetarian-style Parmesan cheese in most major supermarkets.

Curried Tofu Burgers

Serves 4
Preparation Time
20 minutes
Cooking Time
6–8 minutes

Per Serving
253 calories
18g fat
(of which 3g saturates)
15g carbohydrate
0.2g salt

Vegetarian
Dairy Free

1 tbsp sunflower oil, plus extra to fry
1 large carrot, finely grated
1 large onion, finely grated
2 tsp coriander seeds, finely crushed (optional)
1 garlic clove, crushed
1 tsp curry paste
1 tsp tomato purée
225g pack firm tofu
25g (1oz) fresh wholemeal breadcrumbs
25g (1oz) mixed nuts, finely chopped
plain flour to dust
salt and ground black pepper
rice and green vegetables to serve

1 Heat the oil in a large frying pan. Add the carrot and onion and fry for 3–4 minutes until the vegetables are softened, stirring all the time. Add the coriander seeds, if using, the garlic, curry paste and tomato purée. Increase the heat and cook for 2 minutes, stirring all the time.

2 Put the tofu into a bowl and mash with a potato masher. Stir in the vegetables, breadcrumbs and nuts and season with salt and pepper. Beat thoroughly until the mixture starts to stick together. With floured hands, shape the mixture into eight burgers.

3 Heat some oil in a frying pan and fry the burgers for 3–4 minutes on each side until golden brown. Alternatively, brush lightly with oil and cook under a hot grill for about 3 minutes on each side or until golden brown. Drain on kitchen paper and serve hot, with rice and green vegetables.

Couscous-stuffed Mushrooms

Serves 4

Preparation Time
3 minutes

Cooking Time
about 12 minutes

Per Serving

373 calories

25g fat

(of which 10g saturates)

25g carbohydrate

0.6g salt

Vegetarian

125g (4oz) couscous
20g pack fresh flat-leafed parsley,
roughly chopped
280g jar mixed antipasti in oil,
drained and oil put to one side
8 large flat portabellini mushrooms
25g (1oz) butter
25g (1oz) plain flour
300ml (½ pint) skimmed milk
75g (3oz) mature vegetarian Cheddar,
grated, plus extra to sprinkle
green salad to serve

1 Preheat the oven to 220°C (200°C fan oven) mark 7. Put the couscous into a bowl with 200ml (7fl oz) boiling water, the parsley, antipasti and 1 tbsp of the reserved oil. Stir well.

2 Put the mushrooms on a non-stick baking tray and spoon a little of the couscous mixture into the centre of each. Cook in the oven while you make the sauce.

3 Whisk together the butter, flour and milk in a small pan over a high heat until the mixture comes to the boil. Reduce the heat as soon as it starts to thicken, then whisk constantly until smooth. Take the pan off the heat and stir in the cheese.

4 Spoon the sauce over the mushrooms and sprinkle with the remaining cheese. Put back into the oven for a further 7–10 minutes until golden. Serve with a green salad.

Broad Bean & Feta Salad

Serves 2

Preparation Time
10 minutes

Cooking Time
5 minutes

Per Serving
197 calories
16g fat
(of which 4g saturates)
5g carbohydrate
1.3g salt

Vegetarian

225g (8oz) podded broad beans (see Cook's Tips)
100g (3½oz) feta cheese, chopped
2 tbsp freshly chopped mint
2 tbsp extra virgin olive oil
a squeeze of lemon juice
lemon wedges to serve (optional)
salt and ground black pepper

1 Cook the beans in salted boiling water for 3–5 minutes until tender. Drain, then plunge into cold water and drain again. Remove their skins if you like (see Cook's Tips).

2 Tip the beans into a bowl, add the feta, mint, oil and a squeeze of lemon juice. Season well with salt and pepper and toss together. Serve with lemon wedges, if you like.

Cook's Tips

For this quantity of broad beans, you will need to buy about 750g (1½lb) beans in pods. Choose small pods, as the beans will be young and will have a better flavour than bigger, older beans.

Very young broad beans, less than 7.5cm (3in) long, can be cooked in their pods and eaten whole. Pod older beans and skin them to remove the outer coat, which toughens with age. To do this, slip the beans out of their skins after blanching. Allow about 250g (9oz) weight of whole beans in pods per person. Unless tiny, remove the beans from their pods. Cook in boiling salted water for 8–10 minutes until tender. Skin if necessary. Serve with melted butter and herbs. Older beans can be made into soup or puréed.

Chilli Bean Cake

Serves 4	3 tbsp olive oil
Preparation Time	75g (3oz) wholemeal breadcrumbs
10 minutes	1 bunch of spring onions, finely chopped
Cooking Time	1 orange pepper, seeded and chopped
20 minutes	1 small green chilli, seeded and finely chopped
	(see Cook's Tips)
Per Serving	1 garlic clove, crushed
265 calories	1 tsp ground turmeric (optional)
6g fat	400g can mixed beans, drained and rinsed
(of which 1g saturates)	3 tbsp mayonnaise
41g carbohydrate	a small handful of fresh basil, chopped
2.1g salt	salt and ground black pepper
Vegetarian	**To serve**
Dairy Free	soured cream
	freshly chopped coriander
	lime wedges (optional)

1 Heat 2 tbsp oil in a non-stick frying pan over a medium heat and fry the breadcrumbs until golden and beginning to crisp. Remove and put to one side.

2 Add the remaining oil to the pan and fry the spring onions until soft and golden. Add the orange pepper, chilli, garlic and turmeric, if using. Cook, stirring, for 5 minutes.

3 Tip in the beans, mayonnaise, two-thirds of the fried breadcrumbs and the basil. Season with salt and pepper, mash roughly with a fork, then press the mixture down to flatten and sprinkle with the remaining breadcrumbs. Fry the bean cake over a medium heat for 4–5 minutes until the base is golden. Remove from the heat, cut into wedges and serve with soured cream, coriander and lime wedges, if you like.

Cook's Tips

Chillies vary enormously in strength, from quite mild to blisteringly hot, depending on the type of chilli and its ripeness. Taste a small piece first to check it's not too hot for you.

Be extremely careful when handling chillies not to touch or rub your eyes with your fingers, or they will sting. Wash knives immediately after handling chillies. As a precaution, use rubber gloves when preparing them, if you like.

Macaroni Cheese

Serves 4
Preparation Time
10 minutes
Cooking Time
15 minutes

Per Serving
680 calories
34g fat
(of which 21g saturates)
67g carbohydrate
2g salt

Vegetarian

225g (8oz) short-cut macaroni
50g (2oz) butter
50g (2oz) plain flour
900ml (1½ pints) milk
½ tsp grated nutmeg or mustard powder
225g (8oz) mature vegetarian Cheddar cheese, grated
3 tbsp fresh white or wholemeal breadcrumbs
salt and ground black pepper

1 Cook the macaroni in a large pan of salted boiling water, according to the pack instructions, until al dente.

2 Meanwhile, melt the butter in another pan, stir in the flour and cook, stirring, for 1 minute. Remove from the heat and gradually stir in the milk. Bring to the boil and cook, stirring, until the sauce thickens. Remove from the heat. Season with salt and pepper, and add the nutmeg or mustard.

3 Drain the macaroni and add to the sauce, together with three-quarters of the cheese. Mix well, then turn into an ovenproof dish.

4 Preheat the grill to high. Sprinkle the breadcrumbs and remaining cheese over the macaroni. Put under the hot grill for 2–3 minutes until golden brown on top and bubbling. Serve.

Ribbon Pasta with Courgettes

Serves 4
Preparation Time
about 5 minutes
Cooking Time
8–10 minutes

Per Serving
518 calories
15g fat
(of which 2g saturates)
86g carbohydrate
1.7g salt

Vegetarian
Dairy Free

450g (1lb) pappardelle pasta
2 large courgettes, coarsely grated
1 red chilli, seeded and finely chopped
(see Cook's Tips, page 25)
2 tbsp salted capers, rinsed
1 garlic clove, crushed
4 tbsp pitted black Kalamata olives,
roughly chopped
4 tbsp extra virgin olive oil
2 tbsp freshly chopped flat-leafed
parsley
salt and ground black pepper
freshly grated Parmesan to serve
(see Cook's Tip, page 20)

1 Cook the pappardelle in a large pan of boiling water until al dente. About 1 minute before the end of the cooking time, add the courgettes, then simmer until the pasta is just cooked.

2 Meanwhile, put the chilli, capers, garlic, olives and oil in a small pan. Stir over a low heat for 2–3 minutes.

3 Drain the pasta and put back in the pan. Pour the hot caper mixture on top, mix well and toss with the parsley. Season with salt and pepper and serve immediately with the Parmesan.

Try Something Different
If cooking for non-vegetarians, try this variation. Omit the Parmesan cheese and in step 2, add a 50g can of anchovies, drained and roughly chopped.

Fast Fish Soup

Serves 4
Preparation Time
10 minutes
Cooking Time
15 minutes

Per Serving
269 calories
10g fat
(of which 2g saturates)
6g carbohydrate
0.6g salt

1 leek, finely sliced
4 fat garlic cloves, crushed
3 celery sticks, finely sliced
1 small fennel bulb, finely sliced
1 red chilli, seeded and finely chopped
(see Cook's Tips, page 25)
3 tbsp olive oil
50ml (2fl oz) dry white wine
about 750g (1lb 10oz) mixed fish and shellfish,
such as haddock, monkfish, salmon, raw peeled
prawns and cleaned mussels
4 medium tomatoes, chopped
2 tbsp freshly chopped thyme
salt and ground black pepper

1 Put the leek in a large pan and add the garlic, celery, fennel, chilli and oil. Cook over a medium heat for 5 minutes or until the vegetables are soft and beginning to colour.

2 Stir in 1.1 litres (2 pints) boiling water and the wine. Bring to the boil, then reduce the heat, cover and simmer for 5 minutes.

3 Meanwhile, cut the fish into large chunks. Add to the soup with the tomatoes and thyme. Continue simmering gently until the fish has just turned opaque. Add the prawns and simmer for 1 minute then add the mussels, if you're using them. As soon as all the mussels have opened, season the soup and ladle into warmed bowls. Discard any mussels that remain closed, then serve immediately.

Cook's Tip
Frozen seafood mix is a useful standby. Use it instead of the fish and shellfish in this recipe but take care not to overcook or it will become tough.

Plaice with Herb & Polenta Crust

Serves 2
Preparation Time
15 minutes
Cooking Time
4–6 minutes

Per Serving
376 calories
17g fat
(of which 3g saturates)
19g carbohydrate
0.6g salt

Gluten Free
Dairy Free

1 tsp finely chopped rosemary or 1 tsp finely
snipped chives
1 tsp finely chopped thyme
2 garlic cloves, very finely chopped
50g (2oz) polenta
finely grated zest and juice of 2 small lemons
2 plaice fillets, about 175g (6oz) each, skinned
1 large egg
2 tbsp olive oil
salt and ground black pepper
roasted tomatoes, green beans and lemon
wedges to serve

1 Combine the herbs, garlic and polenta on a flat plate. Add the lemon zest, salt and pepper and mix well. Wipe the plaice fillets with kitchen paper.

2 Beat the egg in a shallow dish, dip the fish fillets in the egg and coat them with the polenta mixture, pressing it on well.

3 Heat the oil in a very large frying pan over a high heat. When hot, add the fish, reduce the heat to medium and cook for 2–3 minutes on each side, depending on the thickness of the fillets. Drain on kitchen paper. Serve with lemon juice poured over them, with roasted tomatoes, green beans and extra lemon wedges.

Quick Crab Cakes

Serves 4

Preparation Time

15 minutes

Cooking Time

6 minutes

Per Serving

124 calories

4g fat

(of which 1g saturates)

12g carbohydrate

0.9g salt

Dairy Free

200g (7oz) fresh crabmeat
2 spring onions, finely chopped
2 red chillies, seeded and finely chopped
(see Cook's Tips, page 25)
finely grated zest of 1 lime
4 tbsp freshly chopped coriander
about 40g (1½oz) wholemeal breadcrumbs
1 tbsp groundnut oil
1 tbsp plain flour
salt and ground black pepper
thinly sliced red chilli, seeded, to garnish
1 lime, cut into wedges, and salad leaves to serve

1 Put the crabmeat in a bowl, then mix with the spring onions, chillies, lime zest, coriander and seasoning. Add enough breadcrumbs to hold the mixture together, then form into four small patties.

2 Heat ½ tbsp oil in a pan. Dredge the patties with flour and fry on one side for 3 minutes. Add the remaining oil, then turn the patties over and fry for a further 2-3 minutes. Garnish the crab cakes with thinly sliced red chilli and serve with lime wedges to squeeze over them, and salad leaves.

Waste Not
Use leftover bread to make breadcrumbs and freeze – a great timesaver. You can use them from frozen.

Pesto Cod with Butter Beans

Serves 4
Preparation Time
5 minutes
Cooking Time
15 minutes

Per Serving
403 calories
16g fat
(of which 3g saturates)
24g carbohydrate
2.5g salt

Gluten Free

4 cod fillets, about 150g (5oz) each
4 tbsp red pepper pesto
2 tbsp olive oil
2 × 400g cans butter beans, drained and rinsed
2 garlic cloves, crushed
225g (8oz) fresh spinach
a squeeze of lemon juice
salt and ground black pepper

1 Preheat the grill to medium. Spread each cod fillet evenly with 1 tbsp red pesto and grill for 10–15 minutes until the flesh is opaque and just cooked.

2 Meanwhile, heat the oil in a pan and add the butter beans and garlic. Cook for 10 minutes, stirring occasionally and mashing the beans lightly as they warm through. Season with salt and pepper.

3 About 2–3 minutes before serving, add the spinach to the pan and allow it to wilt. Spoon the butter beans on to four warmed plates and top with the cod and any juices from grilling. Squeeze a little lemon juice over each piece of fish and serve immediately.

Fish Goujons

Serves 4
Preparation Time
15 minutes
Cooking Time
10 minutes

Per Serving
267 calories 15g fat
(of which 2g saturates)
10g carbohydrate
0.6g salt

450g (1lb) hake fillets, skinned, boned and
cut into 20 even-sized pieces
1 medium egg, beaten
50g (2oz) fresh breadcrumbs
vegetable oil for deep-frying
Tartare Sauce to serve (see Cook's Tip)

1 Coat the fish pieces in egg, then in the breadcrumbs.

2 Heat the oil in a deep-fat fryer to 180°C (test by frying a small cube of bread; it should brown in 40 seconds), add the fish and fry until golden. Drain on kitchen paper.

3 Serve the goujons on cocktail sticks with the sauce handed separately.

Try Something Different
Other firm fish such as haddock, coley, cod, monkfish and huss can be cooked in the same way.

Cook's Tip
Tartare Sauce Put 150ml (¼ pint) mayonnaise, 1 tsp freshly chopped tarragon or snipped chives, 2 tsp chopped capers, 2 tsp chopped gherkins, 2 tsp freshly chopped parsley and 1 tbsp lemon juice or tarragon vinegar into a bowl and mix well. Leave to stand for at least 1 hour before serving, to allow the flavours to blend. Makes 150ml (¼ pint).

Saffron Paella

Serves 6	
Preparation Time	
5 minutes	
Cooking Time	
20 minutes	
Per Serving	
609 calories	
22g fat	
(of which 6g saturates)	
59g carbohydrate	
1.5g salt	
Dairy Free	

½ tsp saffron threads
900ml–1.1 litres (1½–2 pints) hot chicken stock
5 tbsp olive oil
2 × 70g packs sliced chorizo sausage
6 boneless, skinless chicken thighs, each cut into three pieces
1 large onion, chopped
4 large garlic cloves, crushed
1 tsp paprika
2 red peppers, seeded and sliced
400g can chopped tomatoes in tomato juice

350g (12oz) long-grain rice
200ml (7fl oz) dry sherry
500g pack ready-cooked mussels
200g (7oz) cooked tiger prawns, drained
juice of ½ lemon
salt and ground black pepper
fresh flat-leafed parsley sprigs to garnish (optional)
lemon wedges to serve

1 Add the saffron to the hot stock and leave to infuse for 30 minutes. Meanwhile, heat half the oil in a large heavy-based frying pan. Add half the chorizo and fry for 3–4 minutes until crisp. Remove with a slotted spoon and drain on kitchen paper. Repeat with the remaining chorizo, then put to one side.

2 Heat 1 tbsp oil in the pan, add half the chicken and cook for 3–5 minutes until pale golden brown. Remove from the pan and put to one side. Cook the remaining chicken and put to one side.

3 Reduce the heat slightly, heat the remaining oil and add the onion. Cook for 5 minutes or until soft. Add the garlic and paprika and cook for 1 minute. Put the chicken back into the pan, then add the peppers and the tomatoes.

4 Stir the rice into the pan, then add one-third of the stock and bring to the boil. Season with salt and pepper, reduce the heat and simmer, uncovered, stirring continuously until most of the liquid has been absorbed.

5 Add the remaining stock, a little at a time, allowing the liquid to become absorbed after each addition (this should take about 25 minutes). Add the sherry and cook for a further 2 minutes.

6 Add the mussels and their juices to the pan with the prawns, lemon juice and reserved chorizo. Cook for 5 minutes to heat through. Adjust the seasoning and garnish with the parsley, if you like, and serve with lemon wedges.

Mussel & Potato Stew

Serves 4

Preparation Time
15 minutes

Cooking Time
15 minutes

Per Serving
470 calories
23g fat
(of which 11g saturates)
42g carbohydrate
2.8g salt

Gluten Free

25g (1oz) butter
200g (7oz) rindless back bacon rashers,
cut into strips
700g (1½lb) white potatoes, cut into large chunks
200g can sweetcorn, drained
1kg (2¼lb) mussels, scrubbed, rinsed and beards
removed (see Cook's Tip)
150ml (¼ pint) single cream
1 tbsp freshly chopped flat-leafed parsley
salt and ground black pepper

1 Melt the butter in a large pan, add the bacon and cook, stirring, until the strips separate. Add the potatoes and 150ml (¼ pint) water and season lightly with salt and pepper. Cover with a tight-fitting lid and cook for 10 minutes or until the potatoes are almost tender.

2 Add the sweetcorn and mussels to the pan, cover and bring to the boil, then reduce the heat and simmer for 2–3 minutes until the mussels open; discard any mussels that don't open. Add the cream and chopped parsley and serve immediately.

Cook's Tip
To make sure mussels are safe to eat, check them carefully for cracks and split shells before cooking. Discard these, and any that do not close when tapped sharply. Any mussels that remain closed after cooking should also be thrown away.

Scallops with Ginger

Serves 4
Preparation Time
15 minutes
Cooking Time
3 minutes

Per Serving
197 calories
7g fat
(of which 1g saturates)
6g carbohydrate
2g salt

Dairy Free

2 tbsp vegetable oil
500g (1lb 2oz) shelled large scallops,
cut into 5mm (¼in) slices
4 celery sticks, sliced diagonally
1 bunch of spring onions, sliced diagonally
25g (1oz) piece fresh root ginger, peeled and sliced
2 large garlic cloves, sliced
¼ tsp chilli powder
2 tbsp lemon juice
2 tbsp light soy sauce
3 tbsp freshly chopped coriander
salt and ground black pepper

1 Heat the oil in a wok or large frying pan. Add the scallops, celery, spring onions, ginger, garlic and chilli powder and stir-fry over a high heat for 2 minutes or until the vegetables are just tender.

2 Pour in the lemon juice and soy sauce, allow to bubble up, then stir in about 2 tbsp chopped coriander and season with salt and pepper. Serve immediately, sprinkled with the remaining coriander.

Poached Salmon

Serves 8
Preparation Time
15 minutes
Cooking Time
see below

Per Serving
675 calories 41g fat
(of which 7g saturates)
0g carbohydrate
0.4g salt

1 salmon
wine or water with lemon and a bay leaf
salt and ground black pepper
lemon slices and chervil or flat-leafed parsley
sprigs to garnish

1 To prepare the salmon, slit the fish along the underside between the head and rear gill opening. Cut out the entrails and discard. Rinse the fish to remove all the blood.

2 Snip off the fins and trim the tail into a neat 'V' shape. Leave the head on, if you like. Pat dry with kitchen paper and weigh the fish before cooking.

3 Fill a fish kettle or large pan with water, or a mixture of water and wine. Bring to the boil, then lower the fish into the kettle or pan. (A piece of muslin wrapped around the salmon will enable it to be lifted out.)

4 Bring the liquid back to the boil, then reduce the heat and simmer for 7–8 minutes per 450g (1lb) if eating hot.

5 If eating cold, bring the liquid back to the boil, then cook for 5 minutes for fish under 3.2kg (7lb), 10–15 minutes for fish over 3.2kg (7lb), leave to cool completely in the liquid, then lift out and remove the skin and bones. Season and garnish with lemon slices and chervil or parsley sprigs.

Try something different
Salmon can also be poached in the oven. Put the fish into a deep roasting tin – it must fit snugly. Preheat the oven to 150°C (130°C fan oven) mark 2. Pour enough water, or water and wine over the fish to three-quarters cover it. Cover tightly with buttered foil. Cook in the oven allowing 10 minutes per 450g (1lb). If serving the fish hot, allow an extra 10 minutes at the end of the cooking time.

Salmon & Bulgur Wheat Pilau

Serves 4
Preparation Time
5 minutes
Cooking Time
20 minutes

Per Serving
323 calories
11g fat
(of which 2g saturates)
30g carbohydrate
1.5g salt

Dairy Free

1 tbsp olive oil
1 onion, chopped
175g (6oz) bulgur wheat
450ml (¾ pint) vegetable stock
400g can pink salmon, drained and flaked
125g (4oz) spinach, roughly chopped
225g (8oz) frozen peas
zest and juice of 1 lemon
salt and ground black pepper

1 Heat the oil in a large pan, add the onion and cook until softened. Stir in the bulgur wheat to coat in the oil, then stir in the stock and bring to the boil. Cover the pan, reduce the heat and simmer for 10–15 minutes until the stock has been fully absorbed.

2 Stir in the salmon, spinach, peas and lemon juice and cook until the spinach has wilted and the salmon and peas are heated through. Season to taste with salt and pepper and sprinkle with lemon zest before serving.

Try Something Different
Instead of salmon, use 200g (7oz) cooked peeled prawns and 200g (7oz) cherry tomatoes.

Smoked Haddock Kedgeree

Serves 4
Preparation Time
10 minutes
Cooking Time
20 minutes

Per Serving
429 calories 20g fat
(of which 11g saturates)
38g carbohydrate
3.1g salt

175g (6oz) long-grain rice
450g (1lb) smoked haddock fillets
2 medium eggs, hard-boiled and shelled
75g (3oz) butter
salt and cayenne pepper
freshly chopped flat-leafed parsley to garnish

1 Cook the rice in a pan of lightly salted fast-boiling water until tender. Drain well and rinse under cold running water.

2 Meanwhile, put the haddock into a large frying pan with just enough water to cover. Bring to simmering point, then simmer for 10–15 minutes until tender. Drain, skin and flake the fish, discarding the bones.

3 Chop one egg and slice the other into rings. Melt the butter in a pan, add the cooked rice, fish, chopped egg, salt and cayenne pepper and stir over a medium heat for 5 minutes or until hot. Pile on to a warmed serving dish and garnish with parsley and the sliced egg.

Special Prawn Fried Rice

Serves 4
Preparation Time
5 minutes
Cooking Time
10–13 minutes

Per Serving
412 calories
18g fat
(of which 3g saturates)
46g carbohydrate
1.9g salt

Dairy Free

2 × 250g packs of microwavable rice
(see Cook's Tips)
1 tbsp sesame oil
6 tbsp nasi goreng paste (see Cook's Tips)
200g (7oz) green cabbage, shredded
250g (9oz) cooked and peeled large prawns
2 tbsp light soy sauce
1 tbsp sunflower oil
2 medium eggs, beaten
2 spring onions, thinly sliced
1 lime, cut into wedges, to serve

1 Cook the rice according to the pack instructions.

2 Heat the sesame oil in a wok and fry the nasi goreng paste for 1–2 minutes. Add the cabbage and stir-fry for 2–3 minutes. Add the prawns and stir briefly, then add the rice and soy sauce and cook for a further 5 minutes, stirring occasionally.

3 To make the omelette, heat the sunflower oil in a non-stick frying pan (about 25.5cm/10in in diameter) and add the eggs. Swirl around to cover the base of the pan in a thin layer and cook for 2–3 minutes until set.

4 Roll up the omelette and cut it into strips. Serve the rice scattered with the omelette and spring onions and pass round the lime wedges to squeeze over it.

Cook's Tips
If you can't find microwavable rice, use 200g (7oz) long-grain rice, cooked according to the pack instructions – but do not overcook. Rinse in cold water and drain well before you begin the recipe.
Nasi goreng is a spicy Indonesian dish traditionally eaten for breakfast. Nasi goreng paste can be bought at most large supermarkets and Asian food shops.

Tuna with Coriander Rice

Serves 4
Preparation Time
10 minutes
Cooking Time
about 5 minutes

Per Serving
609 calories
15g fat
(of which 4g saturates)
51g carbohydrate
0.6g salt

Gluten Free
Dairy Free

250g (9oz) basmati rice
8 × 125g (4oz) tuna steaks
5cm (2in) piece fresh root ginger,
peeled and grated
1 tbsp olive oil
100ml (3½fl oz) orange juice
300g (11oz) pak choi, roughly chopped
a small handful of freshly chopped
coriander
ground black pepper
lime wedges to garnish

1 Cook the rice according to the pack instructions.

2 Meanwhile, put the tuna steaks in a shallow dish. Add the ginger, oil and orange juice and season well with pepper. Turn the tuna over to coat.

3 Heat a non-stick frying pan until really hot. Add four tuna steaks and half the marinade and cook for 1–2 minutes on each side until just cooked. Repeat with the remaining tuna and marinade. Remove the fish from the pan and keep warm.

4 Add the pak choi to the frying pan and cook for 1–2 minutes until wilted. When the rice is cooked, drain and stir the coriander through it. Serve the tuna with the pak choi, rice and pan juices and garnish with lime wedges.

Cook's Tip
Basmati rice should be washed before cooking to remove excess starch and to give really light, fluffy results.

Zingy Fish One-pan

Serves 4
Preparation Time
10 minutes
Cooking Time
10–12 minutes

Per Serving
228 calories
7g fat
(of which 1g saturates)
11g carbohydrate
0.5g salt

Dairy Free

125g (4oz) tenderstem broccoli, halved lengthways
250g (9oz) fine asparagus
4 × 125g (4oz) skinless, boneless white fish fillets,
  such as haddock, pollock, cod or coley, ideally
  sustainably caught
50ml (2fl oz) white wine
1 orange, cut into 8 wedges
75g (3oz) sourdough bread, torn into pieces
2 tbsp olive oil
salt and ground black pepper
rice or salad to serve

1 Preheat the oven to 220°C (200°C fan) mark 7. Spread
the broccoli and asparagus in an even layer in a
medium roasting tin. Lay the fish fillets on top and pour
over the wine. Tuck the orange wedges and bread around
the fish. Drizzle over the oil and season well.

2 Cook in the oven for 10–12 minutes, or until the fish
is cooked through and the vegetables are just tender
(they should still have bite). Serve with rice or salad.

Spaghetti alla Carbonara

Serves 4
Preparation Time
10 minutes
Cooking Time
10 minutes

Per Serving
750 calories 38g fat
(of which 12g saturates)
74g carbohydrate
2.2g salt

2 tbsp olive oil
25g (1oz) butter
125–150g (4–5oz) smoked pancetta (see Cook's
Tips), rind removed, cut into strips
1 garlic clove, halved
3 medium eggs
2 tbsp dry white wine
40g (1½oz) freshly grated Parmesan
40g (1½oz) freshly grated Pecorino cheese
400g (14oz) dried spaghetti
salt and ground black pepper
2 tbsp freshly chopped parsley to garnish

1 Heat the oil and butter in a heavy-based pan. Add the pancetta and garlic, and cook over a medium heat for 3–4 minutes until the pancetta begins to crisp. Turn off the heat; discard the garlic.

2 Meanwhile, in a bowl, beat the eggs with the white wine and half each of the cheeses. Season with salt and pepper.

3 Cook the spaghetti in a large pan of boiling salted water according to the pack instructions until it is al dente.

4 When the spaghetti is almost cooked, gently reheat the pancetta in the pan.

5 Drain the spaghetti thoroughly, then return to the pan. Immediately add the egg mixture together with the pancetta. Take the pan off the heat and toss well; the eggs will cook in the residual heat to form a light creamy sauce. Add the remaining cheeses, toss lightly and serve garnished with parsley.

Cook's Tips
If smoked pancetta is unobtainable, use smoked bacon instead, increasing the quantity to 175–225g (6–8oz).
If Pecorino is unobtainable, just double the quantity of the Parmesan.

Italian Sausage Stew

Serves 4

Preparation Time
10 minutes

Cooking Time
15 minutes

Per Serving
443 calories
35g fat
(of which 12g saturates)
6g carbohydrate
3.4g salt

Dairy Free

25g (1oz) dried porcini mushrooms
300g (11oz) whole rustic Italian salami
sausages, such as salami Milano
2 tbsp olive oil
1 onion, sliced
2 garlic cloves, chopped
1 small red chilli, seeded and chopped
(see Cook's Tips, page 25)
1 rosemary sprig
400g can chopped tomatoes
200ml (7fl oz) red wine
ground black pepper
freshly chopped flat-leafed parsley to garnish
tagliatelle or fettucine to serve

1 Put the dried mushrooms in a small bowl, pour on 100ml (3½fl oz) boiling water and leave to soak for 20 minutes, or soften in the microwave on full power for 3½ minutes and leave to cool. Cut the salami into 1cm (½in) slices and put to one side.

2 Heat the oil in a pan, add the onion, garlic and chilli and fry gently for 5 minutes. Meanwhile, strip the leaves from the rosemary sprig and add them to the pan, stirring. Add the salami and fry for 2 minutes on each side or until browned. Drain and chop the mushrooms and add them to the pan. Stir in the chopped tomatoes and red wine, then season with pepper. Simmer, uncovered, for 5 minutes. Sprinkle with parsley and serve with tagliatelle or fettucine.

Herb Sausages with Mustard Dip

Serves 4
Preparation Time
10 minutes
Cooking Time
11 minutes

Per Serving
836 calories
76g fat
(of which 23g saturates)
16g carbohydrate
5g salt

Dairy Free

12 sausages
12 rashers smoked streaky bacon
2 tbsp fresh thyme leaves
4 tbsp wholegrain mustard
8 tbsp mayonnaise
250g (9oz) small tomatoes
salt and ground black pepper

1 Put the sausages in a pan of boiling water, bring back to the boil, reduce the heat and simmer gently for 3 minutes, then drain and leave to cool. Wrap each cold sausage in a rasher of stretched bacon sprinkled with thyme leaves (so the thyme sits next to the sausage) and spear with a wet cocktail stick to secure.

2 Mix together the mustard and mayonnaise and season to taste with salt and pepper.

3 Preheat the barbecue or grill. Cook the sausages for 7–8 minutes until well browned. Barbecue or grill the tomatoes for about 1 minute or until the skins begin to blister and burst.

4 Remove the cocktail sticks from the sausages and serve with the mustard dip and grilled tomatoes.

Try Something Different
You can use any sturdy fresh aromatic herb: oregano or rosemary would make good alternatives to thyme.

Pork Stir-fry with Chilli & Mango

Serves 1

Preparation Time
5 minutes

Cooking Time
10 minutes

Per Serving
550 calories
15g fat
(of which 4g saturates)
67g carbohydrate
3.1g salt

Dairy Free

75g (3oz) medium egg noodles
1 tsp groundnut oil
½ red chilli, seeded and finely chopped
(see Cook's Tips, page 25)
125g (4oz) pork stir-fry strips
1 head pak choi, roughly chopped
1 tbsp soy sauce
½ ripe mango, peeled, stoned and sliced

1 Cook the egg noodles in boiling water according to the pack instructions. Drain, then plunge into cold water and put to one side.

2 Meanwhile, put the oil into a wok or large frying pan and heat until very hot. Add the chilli and pork, and stir-fry for 3–4 minutes. Add the pak choi and soy sauce, and cook for a further 2–3 minutes. Add the mango and toss to combine.

3 Drain the noodles and add to the pan. Toss well and cook for 1–2 minutes until heated through. Serve immediately.

Cook's Tip
The smaller the chilli, the hotter it is.

Pork Chops with Apple Mash

Serves 4
Preparation Time
5 minutes
Cooking Time
about 15 minutes

Per Serving
532 calories 26g fat
(11g saturates)
37g carbohydrate
1.6g salt

4 large potatoes, chopped
4 tsp ready-made spice mix
4 pork chops
25g (1oz) butter
a knob of butter
1 red apple, cored and chopped
salt and ground black pepper

1 Cook the potatoes in a pan of lightly salted water for 10–12 minutes until tender. Meanwhile, rub the spice mix into the pork chops.

2 Heat the butter in a pan. Add the chops and fry for 5 minutes on each side. Remove from the pan and put on to warm plates. Add a splash of hot water to the pan and swirl the juices around to make a thin gravy. Drain the potatoes.

3 Melt a knob of butter in another pan. Add the chopped apple and fry for 1–2 minutes until starting to soften. Tip the drained potatoes into the pan, season with salt and pepper and mash roughly with the apple. Serve with the chops and gravy.

Pork Steaks with Sage & Parma Ham

Serves 4
Preparation Time
5 minutes
Cooking Time
10 minutes

Per Serving
328 calories
20g fat
(of which 9g saturates)
4g carbohydrate
0.8g salt

Gluten Free

4 pork shoulder steaks, about 150g (5oz) each
4 thin slices Parma ham or pancetta
6 sage leaves
1 tbsp oil
150ml (¼ pint) pure unsweetened apple juice
50g (2oz) chilled butter, diced
squeeze of lemon juice
ground black pepper
steamed cabbage or curly kale and
mashed sweet potatoes to serve

1 Put the pork steaks on a board. Lay a slice of Parma ham or pancetta and a sage leaf on each pork steak, then secure to the meat with a wooden cocktail stick. Season with pepper.

2 Heat the oil in a large heavy-based frying pan and fry the pork for about 3–4 minutes on each side until golden brown.

3 Pour in the apple juice, stirring and scraping up the sediment from the base of the pan. Let the liquid bubble until reduced by half. Lift the pork out on to a warmed plate.

4 Return the pan to the heat, add the butter and swirl until melted into the pan juices. Add lemon juice to taste and pour over the pork. Serve with cabbage or curly kale and mashed sweet potatoes.

Try Something Different
Use white wine instead of apple juice.

Cumin-spiced Gammon

Serves 4
Preparation Time
10 minutes
Cooking Time
10 minutes

Per Serving
492 calories
18g fat
(of which 5g saturates)
3g carbohydrate
13.8g salt

Gluten Free
Dairy Free

large pinch each of ground cumin
and paprika
2 tbsp olive oil
2 tsp light muscovado sugar
8 thin smoked gammon steaks,
about 125g (4oz) each
2 large ripe papayas
zest and juice of 2 limes
½ red chilli, seeded and finely chopped
(see Cook's Tips, page 25)
20g (¾oz) fresh mint, finely chopped
steamed green beans to serve

1 Preheat the grill. In a small bowl, mix together the cumin, paprika, oil and half the sugar. Put the gammon on to a non-stick baking sheet, then brush the spiced oil over each side.

2 Grill the gammon for about 5 minutes on each side, basting once or twice with the juices.

3 Meanwhile, cut each papaya in half, then seed and peel. Roughly chop half the flesh and put into a bowl. Purée the remaining fruit with the lime juice. Add to the bowl with the lime zest, chilli, mint and remaining sugar. Spoon the mixture on top of the gammon and serve with green beans.

Curry Pork Steak with Fruit Couscous

Serves 4

Preparation Time
10 minutes

Cooking Time
12–13 minutes

Per Serving
592 calories
31g fat
(of which 8g saturates)
46g carbohydrate
1.4g salt

Dairy Free

4 × 150g (5oz) pork shoulder steaks
2 tbsp medium-hot curry paste
salt and ground black pepper
150g (5oz) couscous
400g can chickpeas, drained and rinsed
250ml (9fl oz) boiling chicken stock
75g (3oz) sultanas
zest and juice of 1 lime
large handful of fresh parsley, chopped
4 tsp aubergine (brinjal) pickle
green salad to serve

1 Preheat the grill to high. Put the pork steaks on a board, cover with clingfilm and flatten slightly with a rolling pin. Transfer to a bowl, add the curry paste and plenty of seasoning and stir to coat. Arrange the steaks on a non-stick baking tray, then grill for 12–13 minutes, turning once, until golden and cooked through.

2 Meanwhile, put the couscous and chickpeas in a large bowl and pour over the boiling stock. Cover with clingfilm and put to one side for 5 minutes, then use a fork to fluff up. Stir in the sultanas, lime zest and juice and most of the parsley.

3 When the pork is cooked through, spoon 1 tsp aubergine pickle on top of each steak, then garnish with the remaining parsley. Serve the pork with the couscous and a green salad.

Spiced Tikka Kebabs

Serves 4
Preparation Time
10 minutes
Cooking Time
20 minutes

Per Serving
150 calories
5g fat
(of which 1g saturates)
4g carbohydrate
0.3g salt

Gluten Free

2 tbsp tikka paste
150g (5oz) natural yogurt
juice of ½ lime
4 spring onions, chopped
350g (12oz) skinless chicken,
cut into bite-sized pieces
lime wedges to serve

1 Preheat the grill. Put the tikka paste, yogurt, lime juice and chopped spring onions into a large bowl. Add the chicken and toss well. Thread the chicken on to skewers.

2 Grill for 8–10 minutes on each side or until cooked through, turning and basting with the paste. Serve with lime wedges to squeeze over the kebabs.

Cook's Tip
Serve with rocket salad: put 75g (3oz) rocket in a large bowl. Add ¼ chopped avocado, a handful of halved cherry tomatoes, ½ chopped cucumber and the juice of 1 lime. Season with salt and pepper and mix together.

Garlic & Thyme Chicken

Serves 4
Preparation Time
10 minutes
Cooking Time
10–15 minutes

Per Serving
135 calories
6g fat
(of which 1g saturates)
trace carbohydrate
0.2g salt

Gluten Free
Dairy Free

2 garlic cloves, crushed
2 tbsp freshly chopped thyme leaves,
plus extra sprigs to garnish
2 tbsp olive oil
4 chicken thighs
salt and ground black pepper

1 Preheat the barbecue or grill. Mix the garlic with the chopped thyme and oil in a large bowl. Season with salt and pepper.

2 Using a sharp knife, make two or three slits in each chicken thigh. Put the chicken into the bowl and toss to coat thoroughly. Barbecue or grill for 5–7 minutes on each side until golden and cooked through. Garnish with thyme sprigs.

Chicken Fajitas

Serves 4
Preparation Time
10 minutes
Cooking Time
20 minutes

Per Serving
651 calories
23g fat
(of which 8g saturates)
63g carbohydrate
1.6g salt

700g (1½lb) boneless, skinless chicken breasts,
cut into chunky strips
2 tbsp fajita seasoning
1 tbsp sunflower oil
1 red pepper, seeded and sliced
360g jar fajita sauce
1 bunch of spring onions, halved
8 large flour tortillas
150g (5oz) tomato salsa
125g (4oz) guacamole dip
150ml (¼ pint) soured cream

1 Put the chicken breasts into a shallow dish and toss together with the fajita seasoning. Heat the oil in a large non-stick frying pan. Add the chicken and cook for 5 minutes or until golden brown and tender.

2 Add the red pepper and cook for 2 minutes. Pour in the fajita sauce and bring to the boil, then reduce the heat and simmer for 5 minutes or until thoroughly heated. Add a splash of boiling water if the sauce becomes too thick. Stir in the spring onions and cook for 2 minutes.

3 Meanwhile, warm the tortillas in a microwave on full power for 45 seconds, or wrap in foil and warm in a preheated oven at 180°C (160°C fan oven) mark 4 for 10 minutes.

4 Transfer the chicken to a serving dish and take to the table, along with the tortillas, salsa, guacamole and soured cream. Let everyone help themselves.

Stuffed Chicken Breasts

Serves 4

Preparation Time
5 minutes

Cooking Time
20 minutes

Per Serving
297 calories
13g fat
(of which 7g saturates)
trace carbohydrate
1.4g salt

Gluten Free

vegetable oil to oil
150g (5oz) ball mozzarella
4 skinless chicken breasts, about 125g (4oz) each
4 sage leaves
8 slices Parma ham
ground black pepper
new potatoes and spinach to serve

1 Preheat the oven to 200°C (180°C fan oven) mark 6. Lightly oil a baking sheet. Slice the mozzarella into eight, then put two slices on each chicken piece. Top each with a sage leaf.

2 Wrap each piece of chicken in two slices of Parma ham, covering the mozzarella. Season with pepper.

3 Put on the prepared baking sheet and cook in the oven for 20 minutes or until the chicken is cooked through. Serve with new potatoes and spinach.

Cook's Tip
Sage has a strong, pungent taste, so you need only a little to flavour the chicken. Don't be tempted to add more than just one leaf to each chicken breast or it will overpower the finished dish.

Thai Green Curry

Serves 6

Preparation Time
10 minutes

Cooking Time
15 minutes

Per Serving
132 calories
2g fat
(of which 0g saturates)
4g carbohydrate
1.4g salt

Dairy Free

2 tsp vegetable oil
1 green chilli, seeded
and finely chopped
(see Cook's Tips,
page 25)
4cm (1½in) piece fresh
root ginger, peeled and
finely grated
1 lemongrass stalk,
trimmed and cut into
three pieces
225g (8oz) brown-cap
or oyster mushrooms
1 tbsp Thai green
curry paste
300ml (½ pint)
coconut milk

150ml (¼ pint)
chicken stock
1 tbsp Thai fish sauce
1 tsp light soy sauce
350g (12oz) boneless,
skinless chicken
breasts, cut into
bite-size pieces
350g (12oz) cooked
peeled large prawns
fresh coriander sprigs
to garnish
Thai fragrant rice
to serve

1 Heat the oil in a wok or large frying pan, add the chilli, ginger, lemongrass and mushrooms and stir-fry for about 3 minutes or until the mushrooms begin to turn golden. Add the curry paste and fry for a further 1 minute.

2 Pour in the coconut milk, stock, fish sauce and soy sauce and bring to the boil. Stir in the chicken, then reduce the heat and simmer for about 8 minutes or until the chicken is cooked.

3 Add the prawns and cook for a further 1 minute. Garnish with coriander sprigs and serve immediately, with Thai fragrant rice.

Easy Thai Red Curry

Serves 4
Preparation Time
5 minutes
Cooking Time
20 minutes

Per Serving
248 calories
8g fat
(of which 1g saturates)
16g carbohydrate
1g salt

Dairy Free

1 tbsp vegetable oil
3 tbsp Thai red curry paste
4 skinless chicken breasts, about 600g
(1lb 5oz) total weight, sliced
400ml can coconut milk
300ml (½ pint) hot chicken
or vegetable stock
juice of 1 lime, plus lime halves to serve
200g pack mixed baby sweetcorn and
mangetouts
2 tbsp freshly chopped coriander,
plus sprigs to garnish
rice or rice noodles to serve

1 Heat the oil in a wok or large frying pan over a low heat. Add the curry paste and cook for 2 minutes or until fragrant.

2 Add the sliced chicken and fry gently for about 10 minutes or until the chicken is browned.

3 Add the coconut milk, hot stock, lime juice and baby sweetcorn to the pan and bring to the boil. Add the mangetouts, then reduce the heat and simmer for 4–5 minutes until the chicken is cooked. Stir in the chopped coriander, garnish with coriander sprigs and serve immediately with rice or noodles, and lime halves to squeeze over.

Mediterranean Chicken

Serves 4

Preparation Time
5 minutes

Cooking Time
20 minutes

Per Serving
223 calories
7g fat
(of which 1g saturates)
3g carbohydrate
0.2g salt

Gluten Free
Dairy Free

1 red pepper, seeded and chopped
2 tbsp capers
2 tbsp freshly chopped rosemary
2 tbsp olive oil
4 skinless chicken breasts, about 125g (4oz) each
salt and ground black pepper
rice or new potatoes to serve

1 Preheat the oven to 200°C (180°C fan oven) mark 6. Put the red pepper into a bowl with the capers, rosemary and oil. Season with salt and pepper and mix well.

2 Put the chicken breasts into an ovenproof dish and spoon the pepper mixture over the top. Cook in the oven for 15–20 minutes until the chicken is cooked through and the topping is hot. Serve with rice or new potatoes.

Try Something Different
Use chopped black olives instead of the capers.

Lamb Steaks with Mixed Bean Salad

Serves 4
Preparation Time
5 minutes
Cooking Time
10 minutes

Per Serving
545 calories
20g fat
(of which 7g saturates)
30g carbohydrate
1.8g salt

Gluten Free Dairy Free

150g (5oz) sunblush tomatoes in oil
1 garlic clove, crushed
2 rosemary sprigs
4 × 175g (6oz) leg of lamb steaks
½ small red onion, finely sliced
2 × 400g cans mixed beans, drained and rinsed
large handful of rocket
salt and ground black pepper

1 Preheat the grill to high. Drain the sunblush tomatoes, reserving the oil. Put the garlic in a large, shallow dish with 1 tbsp oil from the tomatoes. Strip the leaves from the rosemary sprigs, snip into small pieces and add to the dish. Season with salt and pepper, then add the lamb and toss to coat.

2 Grill the lamb for 3-4 minutes on each side until cooked but still just pink. Meanwhile, roughly chop the tomatoes and put into a pan with the onion, beans, remaining rosemary, rocket and a further 1 tbsp oil from the tomatoes. Warm through until the rocket starts to wilt. Serve the lamb steaks with the bean salad on warmed plates.

Spring Lamb & Flageolet Bean Salad

Serves 4
Preparation Time
5 minutes
Cooking Time
10–20 minutes,
plus resting

Per Serving
535 calories
35g fat
(of which 11g saturates)
17g carbohydrate
1.4g salt

Gluten Free
Dairy Free

2–3 lamb fillets, about 700g (1½lb) in total
1 tbsp Dijon mustard
5 tbsp olive oil
1 tsp freshly chopped parsley
2 garlic cloves
juice of 1 lemon
400g can flageolet or cannellini beans,
drained and rinsed
125g (4oz) frisée lettuce or curly endive
250g (9oz) baby plum or cherry tomatoes,
halved
salt and ground black pepper

1 Rub the lamb fillets with the mustard and season with pepper. Put 1 tbsp oil in a non-stick frying pan and fry the lamb over a medium heat for 5–7 minutes on each side for medium-rare, 8–10 minutes for well done. Remove the lamb, cover and put to one side for 5 minutes. This allows the meat to relax, which makes slicing easier.

2 To make the dressing, put the parsley, garlic, lemon juice and remaining oil into a food processor and whiz for 10 seconds. Alternatively, put the ingredients into a screw-topped jar, screw on the lid and shake to combine.

3 Put the beans, frisée or curly endive and the tomatoes into a bowl, combine with the dressing and season to taste with salt and pepper.

4 Slice the lamb into 1cm (½in) pieces and place on top of the flageolet salad. Serve immediately.

Try Something Different
For a vegetarian alternative, skewer the whole tomatoes on soaked wooden kebab sticks, alternating with small balls of mozzarella cheese. Grill the kebabs and drizzle with 2 tbsp pesto sauce thinned with a little olive oil.

Lamb with Spicy Couscous

Serves 4

Preparation Time
10 minutes

Cooking Time
15 minutes

Per Serving
675 calories
37g fat
(of which 13g saturates)
44g carbohydrate
0.5g salt

2 lamb fillets, about 400g (14oz) each
5 tbsp olive oil
1 aubergine, cut into 1cm (½in) dice
1 tsp ground cumin
½ tsp ground cinnamon
225g (8oz) quick-cook couscous
1 large fresh red chilli, seeded and finely chopped
(see Cook's Tips, page 25)
3 tbsp freshly chopped mint
75g (3oz) raisins, soaked in hot water and drained
salt and ground black pepper
Greek yogurt to serve

1 Trim the lamb fillets, rub in 1 tbsp oil and season well with salt and pepper. Heat a heavy-based non-stick pan, add the lamb and fry for 15 minutes, turning regularly. Remove from the pan and leave to rest for 5 minutes (see Cook's Tip).

2 Meanwhile, toss the aubergine in the cumin and cinnamon, then fry in 2 tbsp oil for 10 minutes or until softened. Prepare the couscous according to the pack instructions, then fluff the grains using a fork. Add the aubergine, chilli, 2 tbsp mint, the raisins and the remaining oil to the couscous. Season well with salt and pepper.

3 To serve, slice the lamb and place on top of the couscous. Drizzle with Greek yogurt, sprinkle with the remaining chopped mint and serve immediately.

Cook's Tip
Leaving the lamb to rest for 5 minutes allows the juices to set and they won't run out.

Crisp Crumbed Lamb Cutlets

Serves 4
Preparation Time
20 minutes
Cooking Time
10 minutes

Per Serving
639 calories 51g fat
(of which 21g saturates)
15g carbohydrate
1.9g salt

75g (3oz) breadcrumbs, made from one-day-old bread
40g (1½ oz) Parma ham, finely chopped
3 tbsp freshly grated Parmesan
8 lamb cutlets, well trimmed, or 2 French-trimmed racks of lamb, about 350g (12oz) each, divided into cutlets
2 eggs, beaten
3 tbsp oil
3 large garlic cloves, peeled but left whole
salt and ground black pepper
tomato relish, new potatoes and a salad or green vegetable to serve

1 Mix together the breadcrumbs, Parma ham and Parmesan, spread out on a large plate and put to one side.

2 Season the lamb with salt and pepper, and brush lightly with beaten egg. Press the lamb into the breadcrumbs to coat evenly, but lightly.

3 Heat the oil in a large non-stick frying pan, add the peeled garlic cloves and heat gently until golden brown, then discard the garlic.

4 Fry the lamb in the garlic-infused oil over a low-medium heat for 4–5 minutes on each side until deep golden brown and crisp. Turn and fry the fat edge for 1–2 minutes.

5 Serve the cutlets with tomato relish, new potatoes and a salad or green vegetable.

Lamb Chops with Crispy Garlic Potatoes

Serves 4
Preparation Time
10 minutes
Cooking Time
20 minutes

Per Serving
835 calories
45g fat
(of which 19g saturates)
22g carbohydrate
0.7g salt

Gluten Free
Dairy Free

2 tbsp Mint Sauce (see Cook's Tips)
8 small lamb chops
3 medium potatoes, cut into 5mm (¼in) slices
2 tbsp Garlic-infused Olive Oil (see Cook's Tips)
1 tbsp olive oil
salt and ground black pepper
steamed green beans to serve

1 Spread the mint sauce over the lamb chops and leave to marinate while you prepare the potatoes.

2 Boil the potatoes in a pan of lightly salted water for 2 minutes or until just starting to soften. Drain, tip back into the pan and season, then add the garlic oil and toss to combine.

3 Meanwhile, heat the olive oil in a large frying pan and fry the chops for 4–5 minutes on each side until just cooked, adding a splash of boiling water to the pan to make a sauce. Remove the chops and sauce from the pan and keep warm.

4 Add the potatoes to the pan. Fry over a medium heat for 10–12 minutes until crisp and golden. Divide the potatoes, chops and sauce among four warmed plates and serve with green beans.

Cook's Tips
Mint Sauce Finely chop 20g (¾oz) fresh mint and mix with 1 tbsp each olive oil and white wine vinegar.
Garlic-infused Olive Oil Gently heat 2 tbsp olive oil with peeled sliced garlic for 5 minutes and use immediately. Do not store.

Quick Beef Stroganoff

Serves 4
Preparation Time
10 minutes
Cooking Time
20 minutes

Per Serving
750 calories
60g fat
(of which 35g saturates)
3g carbohydrate
0.5g salt

Gluten Free

700g (1½lb) rump or fillet steak, trimmed
50g (2oz) unsalted butter or 4 tbsp olive oil
1 onion, thinly sliced
225g (8oz) brown-cap mushrooms, sliced
3 tbsp brandy
1 tsp French mustard
200ml (7fl oz) crème fraîche
100ml (3½fl oz) double cream
3 tbsp freshly chopped flat-leafed parsley
salt and ground black pepper
rice or noodles to serve

1 Cut the steak into strips about 5mm (¼in) wide and 5cm (2in) long.

2 Heat half the butter or oil in a large heavy frying pan over a medium heat. Add the onion and cook gently for 10 minutes or until soft and golden. Remove with a slotted spoon and put to one side. Add the mushrooms to the pan and cook, stirring, for 2–3 minutes until golden brown. Remove and put to one side.

3 Increase the heat and and add the remaining butter or oil to the pan. Quickly fry the meat, in two or three batches, for 2–3 minutes, stirring constantly to ensure even browning. Add the brandy and allow it to bubble to reduce.

4 Put the meat, onion and mushrooms back into the pan. Reduce the heat and stir in the mustard, crème fraîche and cream. Heat through, stir in most of the parsley and season with salt and pepper. Serve with rice or noodles, with the remaining parsley scattered over the top.

Freezing Tip
To freeze Complete the recipe, transfer to a freezerproof container, cool, label and freeze for up to three months.
To use Thaw overnight in the fridge. Put into a pan, cover and bring to the boil, then reduce the heat to low and simmer until piping hot.

Sesame Beef

Serves 4	2 tbsp soy sauce
Preparation Time	2 tbsp Worcestershire sauce
10 minutes	2 tsp tomato purée
Cooking Time	juice of ½ lemon
10 minutes	1 tbsp sesame seeds
	1 garlic clove, crushed
Per Serving	400g (14oz) rump steak, sliced
207 calories	1 tbsp vegetable oil
10g fat	3 small pak choi, chopped
(of which 3g saturates)	1 bunch spring onions, sliced
4g carbohydrate	freshly cooked egg noodles or tagliatelle to serve
2g salt	
Gluten Free	
Dairy Free	

1 In a bowl, mix together the soy sauce, Worcestershire sauce, tomato purée, lemon juice, sesame seeds and garlic. Add the steak and toss to coat.

2 Heat the oil in a large wok or non-stick frying pan until hot. Add the steak and sear well. Remove from the wok and put to one side.

3 Add any sauce from the bowl to the wok and heat for 1 minute. Add the pak choi, spring onions and steak, and stir-fry for 5 minutes. Add freshly cooked and drained noodles or pasta, toss and serve immediately.

Try Something Different
Use 400g (14oz) pork escalope cut into strips instead of beef. Cook for 5 minutes before removing from the pan at step 2.

Sweet Chilli Beef Stir-fry

Serves 4
Preparation Time
10 minutes
Cooking Time
15 minutes

Per Serving
273 calories
13g fat
(of which 5g saturates)
8g carbohydrate
0.2g salt

Gluten Free
Dairy Free

1 tsp chilli oil
1 tbsp soy sauce
1 tbsp clear honey
1 garlic clove, crushed
1 large red chilli, halved, seeded and chopped
(see Cook's Tips, page 25)
400g (14oz) lean beef, cut into strips
1 tsp sunflower oil
1 broccoli head, sliced into small florets
200g (7oz) mangetouts, halved
1 red pepper, halved, seeded and cut into strips

1 Put the chilli oil in a medium-sized shallow bowl. Add the soy sauce, honey, garlic and chilli, and stir well. Add the strips of beef and toss in the marinade.

2 Heat the sunflower oil in a wok over a high heat until it is very hot. Cook the strips of beef in two batches, then remove them from the pan and put to one side and keep warm. Wipe the pan with kitchen paper to remove any residue.

3 Add the broccoli, mangetouts, red pepper and 2 tbsp water. Stir fry for 5–6 minutes until starting to soften. Return the beef to the pan to heat through.

Try Something Different
Other vegetables are just as good: try pak choi, baby sweetcorn, courgettes or carrots cut into thin strips.

Steak au Poivre

Serves 4

Preparation Time
10 minutes

Cooking Time
4–12 minutes

Per Serving
480 calories 35g fat
(of which 19g saturates)
1g carbohydrate
1g salt

2 tbsp black or green peppercorns
4 rump or sirloin steaks, 200g (7oz) each
25g (1oz) butter
1 tbsp oil
2 tbsp brandy
150ml (¼ pint) double cream or crème fraîche
salt
herbed roast potatoes and green beans to serve

1 Crush the peppercorns coarsely using a pestle and mortar or a rolling pin. Scatter the peppercorns on a board, lay the steaks on top and press hard to encrust the surface of the meat; repeat with the other side.

2 Heat the butter and oil in a frying pan and quickly sear the steaks over a high heat. Reduce the heat to medium and cook for a further 3–12 minutes, according to taste, turning every 2 minutes (see Cook's Tip). Season with salt.

3 Remove the steaks from the pan; keep warm. Add the brandy to the pan, remove from the heat and set alight. When the flame dies, stir in the cream or crème fraîche, season and reheat gently. Pour the sauce over the steaks and serve with roast potatoes and green beans.

Try Something Different
Steak Diane Trim 4 pieces of fillet steak, 5mm (¼in) thick, of excess fat. Fry the steaks in 25g (1oz) butter and 2 tbsp vegetable oil for 1–2 minutes on each side. Remove with a slotted spoon and keep warm. Stir 2 tbsp Worcestershire sauce and 1 tbsp lemon juice into the pan juices. Warm through, then add 1 small onion, peeled and grated and 2 tsp freshly chopped parsley, and cook gently for 1 minute. Serve the sauce spooned over the steaks.

COOK'S TIP
Allow 4 minutes (one turn) for rare steaks; 8 minutes (three turns) for medium. For well-done, 12 minutes, increasing the time between turns to 3 minutes.

Cinnamon Pancakes

Serves 6
Preparation Time
5 minutes,
plus standing
Cooking Time
20 minutes

Per Serving
141 calories
5g fat
(of which 1g saturates)
20g carbohydrate
0.1g salt

Vegetarian

150g (5oz) plain flour
½ tsp ground cinnamon
1 medium egg
300ml (½ pint) skimmed milk
olive oil to fry
fruit compote or sugar and Greek yogurt to serve

1 In a large bowl, whisk together the flour, cinnamon, egg and milk to make a smooth batter. Leave to stand for 20 minutes.

2 Heat a heavy-based frying pan over a medium heat. When the pan is really hot, add 1 tsp oil, pour in a ladleful of batter and tilt the pan to coat the base with an even layer. Cook for 1 minute or until golden. Flip over and cook for 1 minute. Repeat with the remaining batter, adding more oil if necessary, to make six pancakes. Serve with a fruit compote or a sprinkling of sugar, and a dollop of yogurt.

Mango Gratin with Sabayon

Serves 6
Preparation Time
5 minutes, plus optional
10 minutes resting
Cooking Time
10 minutes

Per Serving
249 calories
5g fat
(of which 1g saturates)
45g carbohydrate
0g salt

Vegetarian
Dairy Free

3 large ripe mangoes, peeled, stoned and sliced
5 medium egg yolks
6 tbsp golden caster sugar
300ml (½ pint) champagne or sparkling wine
6 tbsp dark muscovado sugar to sprinkle
crisp sweet biscuits to serve

1 Arrange the mangoes in six serving glasses. Whisk the egg yolks and caster sugar in a large heatproof bowl over a pan of gently simmering water until the mixture is thick and falls in soft ribbon shapes. Add the champagne or sparkling wine and continue to whisk until the mixture is thick and foamy again. Remove from the heat.

2 Spoon the sabayon over the mangoes, sprinkle with the muscovado sugar, then leave for 10 minutes to go fudgey. Serve with biscuits.

Quick Gooey Chocolate Puddings

Serves 4
Preparation Time
15 minutes
Cooking Time
12–15 minutes

Per Serving
468 calories
31g fat
(of which 19g saturates)
46g carbohydrate
0.6g salt

Vegetarian

100g (3½oz) unsalted butter,
plus extra to grease
100g (3½oz) golden caster sugar,
plus extra to dust
100g (3½oz) plain chocolate (at least
70% cocoa solids), broken into pieces
2 large eggs
20g (¾oz) plain flour
icing sugar to dust
whipped cream to serve

1 Preheat the oven to 200°C (180°C fan oven) mark 6. Butter four 200ml (7fl oz) ramekins and dust with sugar. Melt the chocolate and butter in a heatproof bowl set over a pan of gently simmering water, making sure the base of the bowl doesn't touch the water. Take the bowl off the pan and leave to cool for 5 minutes.

2 Whisk the eggs, caster sugar and flour together in a bowl until smooth. Fold in the chocolate mixture and pour into the ramekins.

3 Stand the dishes on a baking tray and bake for 12–15 minutes until the puddings are puffed and set on the outside, but still runny inside.

4 Turn out, dust with icing sugar and serve immediately with whipped cream.

Baked Apricots with Almonds

Serves 6
Preparation Time
5 minutes
Cooking Time
20-25 minutes

Per Serving
124 calories
6g fat
(of which 2g saturates)
16g carbohydrate
0.1g salt

Vegetarian
Gluten Free
Dairy Free

12 apricots, halved and stoned
3 tbsp golden caster sugar
2 tbsp amaretto liqueur
25g (1oz) unsalted butter
25g (1oz) flaked almonds
crème fraîche to serve

1 Preheat the oven to 200°C (180°C fan oven) mark 6. Put the apricot halves, cut-side up, in an ovenproof dish. Sprinkle with the sugar, drizzle with the liqueur, then dot each apricot half with a little butter. Scatter the flaked almonds over them.

2 Bake in the oven for 20-25 minutes until the apricots are soft and the juices are syrupy. Serve warm, with crème fraîche.

Try Something Different
Use nectarines or peaches instead of apricots.

Amaretti with Lemon Mascarpone

Serves 4
Preparation Time
15 minutes
Cooking Time
5 minutes

Per Serving
180 calories
8g fat
(of which 4g saturates)
28g carbohydrate
0.4g salt

Vegetarian

finely sliced zest and juice of ¼ lemon
(see Cook's Tips)
1 tbsp golden caster sugar, plus
a little extra to sprinkle
50g (2oz) mascarpone cheese
12 amaretti biscuits

1 Put the lemon juice into a small pan. Add the sugar and dissolve over a low heat. Once the sugar has dissolved, add the lemon zest and cook for 1–2 minutes – it will curl up. Using a slotted spoon, lift out the zest strips and lay them on a sheet of baking parchment, reserving the syrup. Sprinkle the strips with sugar to coat.

2 Beat the mascarpone in a bowl to soften, then stir in the reserved sugar syrup.

3 Put a blob of mascarpone on each amaretti biscuit, then top with a couple of strips of the crystallised lemon peel.

Cook's Tips
To prepare the strips of zest, pare the rind from the lemon, remove any white pith, and finely slice the zest into long strips.
If you're short of time, buy a pack of crystallised lemon slices and use these to decorate the pudding.
Alternatively, decorate each biscuit with a little finely grated lemon zest.

White Chocolate & Berry Crêpes

Serves 4
Preparation Time
2 minutes
Cooking Time
10 minutes

Per Serving
476 calories
37g fat
(of which 15g saturates)
37g carbohydrate
0.2g salt

Vegetarian

500g bag frozen mixed berries, thawed
100g (3½oz) good-quality white chocolate,
broken into pieces
142ml carton double cream
4 thin ready-made crêpes

1 Put the thawed berries into a large pan and cook over a medium heat for 5 minutes or until heated through.

2 Meanwhile, put the chocolate and cream into a heatproof bowl set over a pan of simmering water, making sure the bottom of the bowl doesn't touch the hot water. Heat gently, stirring, for 5 minutes or until the chocolate has just melted. Remove the bowl from the pan and mix the chocolate and cream to a smooth sauce. Alternatively, microwave the chocolate and the cream together on full power for 2–2½ minutes (based on a 900W oven), then stir until smooth.

3 Meanwhile, heat the crêpes according to the pack instructions.

4 To serve, put each crêpe on a warmed plate and fold in half. Spoon a quarter of the berries into the middle of each, then fold the crêpe over the filling and pour the hot chocolate sauce over the top.

Cook's tip
Instead of mixed berries, try using just one type of berry.

Nectarines in Spiced Honey & Lemon

Serves 4
Preparation Time
10 minutes,
plus cooling

Per Serving
95 calories
trace fat
(of which 0g saturates)
23g carbohydrate
0g salt

Vegetarian
Gluten Free
Dairy Free

4 tbsp clear honey
2 star anise
1 tbsp freshly squeezed lemon juice
150ml (¼ pint) boiling water
4 ripe nectarines or peaches, halved and stoned
vanilla ice cream to serve

1 Put the honey, star anise and lemon juice in a heatproof bowl. Stir in the boiling water and leave until just warm.

2 Add the nectarines or peaches to the bowl and leave to cool. Transfer to a glass serving dish. Serve with a scoop of vanilla ice cream.

Try Something Different
Use a cinnamon stick instead of the star anise.

Index

KITCHEN NOTES

Both metric and imperial measures are given for the recipes. Follow either set of measures, not a mixture of both, as they are not interchangeable.

All spoon measures are level.
1 tsp = 5ml spoon; 1 tbsp = 15ml spoon.

Ovens and grills must be preheated to the specified temperature.

Medium eggs should be used except where otherwise specified. Free-range eggs are recommended.

Note that some recipes contain raw or lightly cooked eggs. The young, elderly, pregnant women and anyone with an immune-deficiency disease should avoid these because of the slight risk of salmonella.

Photographers: Steve Baxter (pages 26, 27, 50 and 51); Martin Brigdale (pages 38, 39, 46, 67, 86 and 87); Nicki Dowey (pages 5, 8, 9, 14, 15, 21, 24, 30, 42, 43, 47, 52, 53, 55, 56, 57, 60, 61, 62, 63, 66, 70, 71, 72, 77, 78, 79, 82, 83, 88, 89 and 94); Craig Robertson (pages 6, 7, 25, 33, 36, 37, 64, 65, 68, 69, 73, 75, 76, 84, 85, 90 and 91); Lucinda Symons (pages 12, 13, 16, 17, 18, 19, 20, 22, 23, 28, 29, 31, 32, 34, 35, 40, 41, 44, 45, 54, 74, 80, 81, 92 and 93); Jon Whitaker (pages 10, 11, 48, 49, 58 and 59)

Home Economists: Joanna Farrow, Emma Jane Frost, Teresa Goldfinch, Alice Hart, Lucy McKelvie, Kim Morphew, Bridget Sargeson and Mari Mererid Williams

Stylists: Tamzin Ferdinando, Wei Tang, Helen Trent and Fanny Ward

First published in Great Britain in 2012
by Collins & Brown
10 Southcombe Street
London W14 0RA

An imprint of Anova Books Company Ltd

The Good Housekeeping website is
www.allaboutyou.com/goodhousekeeping

ISBN 978-1-908449-40-5

A catalogue record for this book is available from the British Library.

Reproduction by Dot Gradations Ltd, UK
Printed and bound by 1010 Printing International Ltd, China

This book can be ordered direct from the publisher. Contact the marketing department, but try your bookshop first.

www.anovabooks.com